TAP
YOUR
SOURCE

TAP YOUR SOURCE

Leslie Karen Hammond

Taos Pueblo Press

TAP YOUR SOURCE

Published by: Taos Pueblo Press
              PO Box 178
              Taos, NM 87571

Front Cover Image Copyright Pavelk, 2009. Used under license
from Shutterstock.com.
Back Cover Photo Tom Bombria Photography.

Cover Design by Judy Ricketts-White /
Ricketts-White Design

Interior Design by Kathy Pooler /
Publications Plus

Requests for permissions should be sent to:
Taos Pueblo Press
PO Box 178
Taos, NM 87571
860-303-8772

Printed in the United States of America
ISBN: 978-0-9836344-0-9

Table of Contents

About The Author

Leslie Karen Hammond is a Native American. She is a member of the Taos Pueblo, and has been inducted as a Shaman in the ancient Andean Traditions by the Peruvian Q'echua Natives.

Leslie is also an International Inspirational Speaker, has served as an Area Governor for Toastmasters International, is an associate member of the National Speakers Association, and a Trustee and Board Member for the non-profit - The TSETSE Gallery in New London, CT and a Board Member for the Southeastern CT Women's Network.

She is the consummate networker, an eternal optimist and her mission is to make a difference. Leslie is passionate about everything she does, she inspires others to become leaders in their own right and empowers people to find their purpose. In her opinion there is no greater calling, than to be of service.

As a dynamic award-winning speaker and the principal of her own firm, Leslie Karen Hammond Company, Leslie helps people break through their old patterns of thinking and step into their dreams. Leslie constantly strives to help people bring out the best in themselves while using her experience to inspire a new way of thinking. She brings infectious enthusiasm, professionalism and passion into everything she does.

For recreation and fun, Leslie enjoys in skydiving, fire eating, scuba diving, hot coal walking, horseback riding, traversing the jungles of Peru, hiking in the mountains of Peru, New Mexico and New Hampshire, participating in

Habitat For Humanity's Home Builder Blitz, organic gardening, vegetarian cooking, yoga and commissioned stained glass work. The lessons acquired through Leslie's adventures and experience are creatively woven into her inspirational presentations on "Stepping Out of Your Comfort Zone," "Embracing Change, Taking Your Vision To the Next Level," "The Power of Your Beliefs," "The Wisdom of Surrender."

Leslie lives in New London Connecticut, and travels frequently between Taos, New Mexico and Peru.

Leslie may be reached at: leslie@lesliekarenhammond.com

Acknowledgements

This book is dedicated to my son Josh, Mary Agnes and everyone who has made an impact my life – you know who you are! All my encounters have presented extraordinary opportunities for growth, I am incredibly grateful.

Special thanks to Rick Segel, for sparking the fire, without his encouragement this book may have taken years to come to fruition, many thanks also go out to Nathan Jaycox, Richard Pass, Mark Roberts, Judy Ricketts-White, Kathy Pooler and countless others who have provided their enthusiasm and their support.

Introduction and
"How To" Use This Book

Tap Your Source is a book about discovering your potential and embracing transition. Transition can be a very delicate subject, however, it's something we have all come to know very well at some point in our lives. If you don't think so, consider the last time you changed jobs, spouses or moved into another home. Either we admit we're in transition and are fighting it, or we deny we are in its midst and ignore the opportunity transition can be presenting. I've been in both places-the fighting and the denial, several times in fact; just to be sure I fully understood how to be miserable. Had I realized the gift of transition much earlier, there may have been a little less tension in my life.

All kidding aside, the road to success is paved with the good intentions of those that didn't have the "right tools" to get from Point A-where you are now to Point B, your ultimate destination. Transition can be one of those "right" tools.

The average mindset does not embrace personal transformation when it most needs to be, that is when it's thrust upon you against your will and you're left to your own devices. The key to "embracing with grace", lies within our perception and in our willingness to employ change to work on our behalf. The more we resist transition, the more difficult it becomes. The more we blame others for our circumstance, the more likely we will miss the value in the opportunity we have been given.

More than a rainy day/travel read; this is a work book. Action is required within each chapter to help you gain a deeper insight into your next steps. Success knows no shortcuts. When you chose to invest your time and energy into what could be the biggest break of your life, you'll soon discover how well it pays to honor the process and invest the time in your vision. You are worth every moment spent shaping your future.

This book is about seizing the opportunity of a lifetime.

Imagination is everything.
It is the preview of life's coming attractions.

Albert Einstein

Chapter 1

The Transition Train

What do you think of when you hear the word "transition"? Is it something positive?

When we hear the word "transition", anyone can relate to the concept. If it's not positive, then I'd like to offer some suggestions on how to shift that perception. We live our lives around this very theme of transition whether we accept it or not. Few have learned to tap into the power of it, much less embrace it.

Have I gotten your attention yet?

Often people don't view change as a transition; instead they may call it "life." When it's unpleasant, some call it bad timing, bad luck, or being in the wrong place at the wrong time. My perspective is much more positive, I view change as giving birth to our new selves. What if we could recognize transition as the gift it truly is? With practice this skill can be mastered. Most of us are not programmed to think this way. If we have not developed this way of thinking, chances are some of the people we spend our time with have not either.

In as much as we can allow transition to be painful, stressful, exhausting, heartbreaking, sorrowful, debilitating or frustrating, we can also allow it to be a great teacher. If you want to remain in a slump, then keep feeling sorry for yourself. While you're at it start asking the question "why me?" or begin asking it more often. When you are ready to explore beyond the discomfort of change, consider replacing the word "why" with the word "how". Asking how we can learn and grow from an experience is powerful. Asking why something is happening fuels the archetype of the victim, but asking yourself "how" fuels the archetype of the victor. Which mindset would you rather be in?

There may be a challenge to the implementation of this concept. The key is to practice until it becomes second nature. It also helps to be surrounded with like-minded people.

One thing that's critical to the implementation of this concept is, remembering we have the ability to make up our own minds. It's too easy to assign blame instead of stepping up to the plate and not taking responsibility for our own thoughts and actions. We can be influenced negatively just as easily as we can be influenced positively, if we are not mindful.

Let's do an exercise in behavioral awareness to examine our current thought process as we encounter an unexpected change in our lives.

Think of a situation you are in the midst of or a situation you've just come through and make note of it below:

_____

_____

_____

_____

_____

Describe your initial reaction:

_____

_____

_____

_____

_____

Think of how else you might have reacted to the situation? _____

_____

_____

_____

_____

_____

List one positive outcome as a result of this event, use your imagination if necessary:

_____

_____

_____

_____

_____

What have I learned from this situation?

_____

_____

_____

_____

_____

Did a light bulb come on? Is there an opportunity for some type of cerebral corrective action? It's never too late for an apology, a thank you or for sharing a reflection with someone you trust. This is a chance to make something positive out of an unpleasant experience. Not only will your attitude change the outcome of the situation, it may change another person's life; in some cases it could have the power to save a life. Transition can be viewed as another chance. Our perceptions shift all the time, with every book we read, every program we watch on television or radio show we listen to. What a wonderful opportunity to make the most of a situation – whatever your perceptional shift during transition is, I guarantee there is someone else out there that will also benefit. Having an opportunity to give something back as a way of expressing our gratitude for what we've gained is nothing short of empowering.

Now let's explore this a little further and have some fun with what we've discovered. We are going to celebrate your newfound mindset. I'd like you to think about the last time you did something worthy of the guttural statement "YEAH". I'm talking about when you hold your right arm up in the air, make a fist and pulling it down with gusto like you were grabbing a fist full of life. Maybe your favorite sports team won a championship, perhaps your child scored at a soccer, football or baseball game. Maybe you just won the lotto!

If you're not quite there yet, that's okay. You can still pretend and invoke the power of your imagination! We've planted the seeds for transformation, the seed now needs to be watered and fertilized. This exercise is going to nurture the feeling of accomplishment and make you smile. My intent is to revive the memory of how good it feels when you just can't keep your enthusiasm to yourself. This feeling will begin the germination process and invite further opportunities for progress.

Let's take a few moments and truly celebrate an accomplishment. So often we move onto the next thing without honoring our victories. This is your moment!

Now that you're feeling pretty good, I'd like to share another great "pick me up". When I find myself in a tough emotional spot, there's a gratitude exercise

I find incredibly empowering. Beginning with the letter "A" I state something I am grateful for and I don't stop till I reach the letter "Z". Most of the time once through the alphabet works but for those "special occasions", I may need to do it again. The challenge of the second time is not using the same statements twice as you once again go through the entire alphabet.

At the end of the day I like to ask myself, "Have I taken something positive from a trying or stressful experience to move myself one step closer toward fulfilling my vision?" If I cannot answer yes, then I'll take a moment to reflect on something as simple as my thought process. I find there is usually an opportunity for growth in recognizing how I view myself or the world.

I'd like to share with you something I've learned along my "transition" journey. I've found that transition can be stressful and sometimes painful if I allow it, however I've also discovered transition can be incredibly sweet. I've also learned that maintaining a positive outlook takes a lot of concentrated effort before it becomes second nature!

Through the years, the most significant transitions of my life have not been of my choosing. Although my career shift has been by choice, I realize yours may not be. Do you feel as if someone has altered your plan without your permission? If someone has changed your plan, then you must realize this may very well turn out to be the best thing that's ever happened to you. I believe big things are coming your way. We all get help from our creator, especially when we are not able to help ourselves. Have faith in your future and do not give in to pessimism or apathy! Develop a mindset that enables you to move forward with purpose.

Ultimately, change equals opportunity, in any language.

NOTES

At first dreams seem impossible,
then improbable,
then inevitable.

—Christopher Reeve

Chapter 2

Dare To Dream

How does a person move through their current circumstance into what they've always dreamed of doing or being?

For starters you envision and romanticize a concept. What do *you* think about daydreaming? I'm not talking about a daydream where you catch up on a little sleep or when you've taken on a new lover. I'm talking about the daydream of your life.

How might you make a difference in your life or in the world without any self-imposed limitations? No financial, emotional, mental, spiritual or physical constraint of any sort. Does that sound liberating?

Here's a concept for you-

Repeat out loud after me," I (insert your name here) give myself permission to engage my imagination". That was great! Now let's try it again and declare our intent with a little more enthusiasm, pretend no one is looking. Once more repeat out loud after me, "I (insert your name here) give myself permission to engage my imagination!"

How did that sound? Was it easier the second time? How did that feel? If you think it felt a little foolish, you're in good company. We don't typically make positive declarations out loud with such vigor unless you are a professional speaker. Once you get beyond any feeling of awkwardness, you are entitled to smile, or dare I suggest even giggle. Now consider the realm of possibility you've just opened yourself up to!

When we were children, there were no limitations to what we could accomplish, at least not in our own minds. We had freedom from narrow-mindedness, judgment and fear.

Somewhere along the rite of passage into adulthood, the innocence of our unbound creativity was lost. The face of our departed courage can be found in many circumstances, for example every doubt we heard when expressing a terrific idea to the wrong person. How about every time we compared ourselves to another? And worst of all, how about when we told ourselves we couldn't do something? Well, today is a new day! Get yourself a journal to track your daydreams because we are about to take the excursion of a lifetime.

Let's begin by finding a quiet place where we will not be interrupted for 10 or 15 minutes, perhaps in your car, at the library, at a state park, the beach or even in the shower (with a waterproof journal of course). It's very important to clear your mind of clutter and practice being present in the moment within this gift of time you are granting yourself. Feeling guilt for not doing something else you think you ought to be doing is simply not allowed. If this concept is new to you and you find your thoughts drifting back to reality it's alright- gently bring yourself back and merely begin again. You'll get more proficient with practice, I promise! Attempt to keep your eyes closed, perhaps play some soft background music to block out any distractions, avoiding anything with lyrics.

Once again, let's grant ourselves permission to let go of our current reality for a small window of time. No need to shout this time however become expressive in a firm authoritarian tone. Repeat after me out loud "I (insert your name here) give myself permission to engage my imagination". Now, close your eyes, take a deep breath and capture this moment of stillness. Perceive the message from your creative genius within. As you receive an insight, smile like you have a secret. Be grateful for this newfound idea. Take a few moments and write down your experience, keeping an ongoing log in your journal for future reference.

My first insight:

_____

_____

_____

_____

_____

_____

Your insight may be the missing ingredient to your favorite pasta sauce. It could be a new design for your flower or vegetable garden; it could be your first or next book. It could be the answer to a long standing question about what brings you joy, reigniting passion in your intimate relationship or how to help a friend in crisis. If you are not overflowing with ideas at first, give yourself a break. It may have been a few years since you dared to reach into the depths of your imagination, so be easy on yourself. Remember that practice makes progress, so please consider giving yourself this gift of time again in the very near future.

With practice, you'll find you need smaller windows of time to manifest these creative ideas. Imagine getting to a point when these thoughts come without any preparation! It will happen when you believe it and when you allow it to happen.

Let's up the stakes a little, shall we? I challenge you to use your first insight in the next 24 hours, while it's fresh. Make a declaration to solidify your intent:

I am _____

_____

_____

_____

_____

_____

_____

Complete that sentence with an <u>action</u> to manifest your insight (i.e. to make it happen). Make it manageable, if your insight was to write a book, schedule time to begin writing and write the first page. Now mark your calendar and engage! For example, you may declare "I am going to have my first chapter written on or by (fill in a date)".

As with any tool, the more often it is used, the more broken-in and comfortable it becomes to work with. Don't sell yourself short; the imagination is the most cost effective tool for growth you possess. Use it don't lose it! While you're at it, schedule your next session for imagination awareness.

One of the benefits of using your imagination could be the ability to embrace the concept of "no holds barred". Why not? You've got nothing to lose. While allowing your dream to unfold, be sure to include an extraordinary ending. I'm willing to bet the outcome of your dream will somehow help others. Perhaps you were destined to encourage others to be of service, if by no other means than sharing your stories of self-discovery. You could be inspiring someone else to greatness! One of the best feelings we've experienced is having a sense of accomplishment. Accomplishment has such potential to create contagious enthusiasm.

Another reason it's important to have a final outcome is because we need a goal to work toward. Take this concept you have in your mind and paint the concept with words in your journal. This is your canvas to paint the future you desire, this is your opportunity to bring to life, a dream. This is your time to bring your message, your gift, and your insight to others.

NOTES

*"There are no failures -
just experiences and your reactions to them."*

Tom Krause

Chapter 3

The Art of Inspiration

What "moves" you creatively? This seems like a simple question, yet it is difficult to answer!

What "moves" us depends on the circumstance. Being "moved" while I watch a movie can bring tears to my eyes but may not inspire me with creative writing. I can also be "moved" by witnessing someone's good deed, but again it may not inspire me to put words in a journal or a manuscript. So where does our creativity come from?

I'd like you to consider what kind of mood, atmosphere or activity gets your creative juices flowing. Perhaps you are inspired by the beauty of the natural world, perhaps by the tranquility of a meadow of tall grass swaying in the breeze, or by the glory of a vibrant sunset. If beauty is in the eyes of the beholder, is not inspiration in the mind of the beholder?

Having an understanding of the ideal time to be creative is important – such as setting aside an evening after dinner or a weekend. However please abstain from the notion this is the only opportunity when creative magic may flow, you may be short- changing yourself. For example, if you think you'll perform best in silence but are having a scheduling challenge, then be open minded to finding more windows of opportunity. It is my belief that we set ourselves up for success and for failure merely by the constraints we impose within our thoughts.

Are you having trouble finding that inspiration? You are in good company! However, consider this. Driving a car has become my new "down time". When I hope to give birth to a new idea, I'll keep the radio off and let my thoughts guide me. Life is just waiting to provide us with the answers to what we seek. Taking a leisurely drive into the country allowing myself the freedom to pursue creative thought is a pastime of mine. Depending on the length of the journey, it can feel like running away from the distractions of home. Then I thought of it as running toward a different home, toward the home of my creative self.

If "going for a Sunday drive" seems a bit wasteful or unrealistic to you and you are having a difficult time finding these windows of opportunity, then consider that this may be more important than you think. Chances are your next move, be it career or personal goal, is contingent upon your coming up with some creative "out of the box" ideas. This not only applies to the inception of your ideas but also to staying on track. Schedule time for yourself as you would for a doctor's appointment, put it on the calendar and alert your family that you are not available. Then stick to it. A family emergency ought to be the only thing to break your appointment. When the people in your life begin to understand you are serious about this, it will become easier and easier to do. Label the time as work, and stay committed to yourself. Remain steadfast, because no one else will make you do it. In fact everyone else may distract you. Be committed, be strong, and remember the importance of this gift you are giving to yourself.

Often times reading or listening to motivational speakers are incredibly inspiring. We gravitate toward like-minded people that seem to speak directly to us. From this place of connectedness, I find my own vision nurtured and rest in knowing that I am either on the right path or at least headed in the right direction. We oftentimes need but a minor change in perspective to stay on track or find the next clue to fulfilling our destiny.

Find that inspirational environment that spurs creativity and let it flow out of you!

The places I find the most conducive to creative thought are:

_____

_____

_____

_____

_____

The most creative time of day for me is: _____

_____ _____

_____

_____

I am making _____ (minutes, hours) of creative/inspirational time every _____ (day, week, month).

I realize the importance of this because: _____

_____

_____

_____

_____

My Priority Checklist

- ❏ I have blocked out these windows of time in my schedule

- ❏ I have a backup plan if something comes up

- ❏ I am important enough to keep this commitment

- ❏ I have the location in mind

- ❏ I have a backup location if necessary

NOTES

THE ART OF INSPIRATION

One person with a belief is equal to a

force of 99 who have only interests.

John Stuart Mill

Chapter 4

The Power of Belief

Have you ever begun a day, a conversation or a thought with "I can't"? I'd bet $20 at some point you have. In this chapter we want to shift the focus away from the "I can't" to the "I can" then into the "I am".

Through the imagination exercise you may have discovered something about dreams, something about yourself and the value of "down time". Dreams typically appear to us in one of three ways, in the night subconsciously, while we are awake, as in a daydream consciously, or as our immediate reality. The latter is reserved for those of us who are presently <u>living</u> our dreams, although many of us aspire to be in this category. For anyone that falls into the last category, my hat goes off to you with sincere congratulations. For the rest of us that are in transition from the night dream or the daydream into our "dream" reality, follow me.

Have you ever had a profound shift in your confidence because some took the time to tell you that they believed in you? How long has it been since you made time to extend your belief in another?

For many of us, moving beyond our dreams toward manifesting a new reality requires more than desire alone. It also requires "fuel" to keep going, and maintenance to stay on track and perseverance along the way. If inspiration was the mother, then belief is the grandmother-she is the one who embraces your creativity and infuses you with her vision for your potential.

From experience I can speak to the power of belief. I've had the privilege of being in the right place at the right time to encounter an amazing individual. There was no coincidence in our meeting. The initial conversation was so profound it brought me to tears. He asked the right questions but also the tough questions, calling me and my dreams on the carpet. How are you making this a reality, he asked? Suddenly I realized I was stuck inside the confines of my current belief structure. His belief was the whole universe compared to my belief which was a mere galaxy. As my eyes welled with tears of joy and gratitude I'd realized the reason I had been drawn to this conference and this individual.

I've had people believe in me before, but this was different. First and foremost, I was ready to hear his words. Being ready is so important. We all have the capacity to listen, but having the ability to integrate what is presented into something tangible is an entirely different thing. I felt that everything I had done in my life was preparation for this moment of realization. How often as adults do we have the opportunity to feel like a child receiving a gift? Children do not question a present, they do not wonder about a hidden agenda, they simply light up like the sun and brighten the world. That's what happened to me that day; I began to glow much brighter than usual.

From that point forward I have made it my mission to infuse that same belief into others. My vision is to create an epidemic of inspired individuals that change lives, and make the world a better place.

I believe there are far too many people in the world that have potential that lies dormant due to a lack of belief in their abilities and the appropriate support system. It could also be in part because, these people believed a pessimist who told them their ideas were nonsense or that they couldn't achieve something. If this has happened to you, we've **all** been there, but we need not **stay** there. Lost passion and suppressed creativity are two of the most tragic things befallen on the human race today; please don't let this happen to you.

Fellow believers take your ideas into the world and run with them! I believe in your potential to make an impact on everyone you encounter. I also believe you are ready for a mentor to take you to the next level. As soon as you join me in this perceptional shift the universe will begin to deliver what is needed to aid you in moving forward. As an exercise in comparison, consider instilling your belief in another and watch what happens as they rise to your perceived potential of them.

What do you believe you are capable of? We've all experienced a moment of growth when we least expected it. If someone was to foretell what was about to occur prior to such an event how do you think you would react? Such unplanned growth experiences remind me of advising a child. A young person has such a limited realm of experience to draw from, that it may be hard for them to conceive the possibility that you are presenting. But as we get older, we become a bit more respectful of the advice of others; even though sometimes we take it lightly it is rather profound and speaks volumes to us.

In hindsight, was the doubt you felt derived from fear? Be it a lack of belief in one's own abilities or a lack of belief you'll have the necessary support structure, you have the ability to break through that old paradigm.

It's time to let go of the negativity of the past. In doing so we will begin to realize that all of our experiences have served a purpose. The sooner we discover something positive to come out of a hardship, the closer we come to fulfilling our potential.

When I work with clients during counseling sessions and the time has come to release something that no longer serves them, I remind them that what they let go of had served a purpose in their life. To release with compassion and understanding is a powerful tool for growth no matter what or when you release it. It starts here and now!

Here are a few simple exercises that I've used to release negativity, pain or disappointment:

• Put your thoughts and feelings on a piece of paper, and then burn it.

• Practice forgiveness.

• Find a small object representing this period in your life. Sit with it quietly and imagine the object as a vessel for your negativity, pain or disappointment. Imagine that with your breath, specifically while inhaling that you have the power to gather all that you wish to release from this time period. Your inhalation will be like a vacuum, drawing out these thoughts that no longer serve you. As you exhale, blow these thoughts into the object you've chosen. Repeat this breath exercise as many times as needed to feel a sense of relief and release. If you have the means, dig a hole and bury the object, if not dispose of it by some other means.

• If you live in the city in a condo and do not have a yard or a shovel at your disposal, another way to release is to blow into a feather or a leaf and then release it in the wind.

Today I am releasing:

_____

_____

_____

_____

_____

_____

I am letting this go because:

_____

_____

_____

_____

_____

_____

Consider making the following statement, perhaps saying it out loud and in front of a mirror.

"I understand this is a choice and that I possess the power to let this go and more forward with my life".

Now that you've done some powerful release work, consider the following questions carefully.

What are you capable of? Use the next few lines to write down the possibilities.

I believe I am capable of:

_____

_____

_____

_____

_____

_____

I am capable of this because I am:

_____

_____

_____

_____

_____

_____

Now read this aloud. Find a full length mirror to stand in front of and read it again. Keep repeating this as your new mantra. While you are reciting this, make a note of your body language. Are you standing erect displaying confidence or are your shoulders slightly curled over displaying hesitation or lack of self-confidence?

What does your face say about the conviction of your message? You must first convince yourself. Sometimes we fool others, but from the depths of our psyche we can see beneath our outward mask into our true selves. Chances are great that if you are entertaining monumental change in your life, you've had some experience moving beyond the time and place of self-doubt. Are you an expert yet?

If you are anything like me, then you may need a reminder from time to time and that's ok. We never stop learning along our path of development. Oftentimes when encouraging others we find ourselves stating exactly what we needed to hear ourselves.

Take these statements you have declared and write them on an index card then re-read these statements aloud to yourself daily. Square back your shoulders, hold your chin high, smile then speak with a quiet authority. For comparison, state your mantra with shoulders slouching almost in a cowering position. Notice the difference?

Keep the faith in yourself and the fact that you are sending a positive intent into the universe. You will manifest what you believe you are capable of accomplishing or being. All that's required is an open heart, an open mind, and a knowingness that you have a message to convey, you have lives to change and you will make a difference!

NOTES

If there is no passion in your life, then have you really lived? Find your passion, whatever it may be. Become it and let it become you and you will find great things happen FOR you, TO you and BECAUSE of you.

T. Alan Armstrong

Chapter 5

Embrace Your Gifts

Usually they will just say they are being a "realist". You know who I am talking about.

When we were children, our dreams knew no boundaries, anything was possible! What was your childhood dream? How did you respond when asked "What do you want to be when you grow up?" How do you respond now as an adult? Can you imagine how that childhood dream could have evolved with an ample supply of encouragement?

History is filled with leaders who pursued and fulfilled a dream. I'm willing to bet at least one of your highest aspirations has been squashed by someone who thought they were protecting you! Surround yourself with others who embrace your gifts and encourage you to use them to pursue excellence. How you embrace your gifts can be determined by first examining how gracefully you receive a compliment. When someone pays you a compliment, how do you typically respond?

For the longest time I was not able to simply say "thank you". I'd either downplay my performance or I'd continue with some excuse or explanation of how I could've done better. I'm not sure when this began, but that bad habit lasted for decades. In the last 10 years something shifted and I learned to graciously accept a compliment. It's a great exercise in empowerment! When I choose to embrace someone's kind words, not make excuses and put on a nice smile, I'll then stand confidently and let the other person continue to speak. Sometimes I get another compliment! If this sounds easy, try it sometime. You'll find it's not as simple as it sounds. If you've been explaining away your compliments for years, it's time to begin embracing them – you deserve the acknowledgment. Don't constantly demand perfection from yourself, but rather embrace your progress and continue building upon the gifts you have.

You may not have the mindset of confidence yet that you are worthy of such acknowledgement, but I know it's possible, I've been there. It may be tough to remember where that negative mindset comes from, I couldn't figure it out. I wasn't deprived of enthusiasm or support as a child. I was loved, yet I still could not graciously receive a compliment. By first acknowledging this was a concern and then after a lot of practice, I've been able to change that mindset. There may still be a time or two when I take an extra moment before responding. However if this person has an appreciation for what I have done then why should I doubt them with negative self-talk?

What I'm suggesting here is to grant yourself the gift of grace. I'm proposing an active practice of having confidence in your abilities by accepting recognition and belief in your power to positively influence others with those abilities. For those who may have grown up in large families, you may not have much practice taking a compliment, due to the often implicitly competitive environment. There are many other reasons we may not graciously accept a compliment. Regardless of your history, you have the power to change.

Now let's imagine you've just given a presentation to 20 people. Your intent was to rehearse it several times, but due to other obligations, you couldn't make time. Instead you projected a positive outcome. By doing so you got beyond any anxiety or apprehension prior to your presentation. You also got beyond the feeling that you just threw some things together and it wasn't your best effort. Now fast forward to the end of your presentation and people are applauding. Everyone wants to compliment you personally; they are admiring your knowledge and are already looking forward to hearing your next talk. You may be tempted to confess your little secret - lack of rehearsal time. STOP and smile, people will have no idea what you're thinking. Having a secret is one thing, keeping it is another. You did a great job and deserve every accolade you receive.

I am not recommending that you continue making future presentations under such conditions. My intent was to present a very likely outcome that may result from a potentially uncomfortable circumstance. Moving beyond your doubt enables you to maintain the faith that you possess a valuable gift, which will almost always have an opportunity to be recognized.

Another word of caution, we must strive to not be intimidated by the accomplishments of others by comparing ourselves to them. Rather, embrace the gifts we possess and seek to enhance these gifts... We can learn to be joyful for the accomplishments of others while exploring how we could learn from them to improve ourselves further. We are all uniquely gifted and we all have a purpose for being here. We touch the lives of everyone we encounter. When we appreciate our gifts in the same way we appreciate the gifts of others, we create a nurturing environment around us.

Practice embracing your talent, embodying your vision and realize your potential. I'd encourage you to do the same for your family and friends. We are all sowing the seeds of potential, be it our families, our own, or those of another. I guarantee you'll experience a positive shift in your thinking.

Let's examine the gifts you bring to the world.

Others have told me that I am a great: _____

_____

_____

_____

_____

Others have told me that I have an extraordinary ability to:

_____

_____

_____

_____

_____

My secret gift I have yet to share with the world is _____

_____

_____

_____

_____

Embrace all that you once were, embrace all that you are, and, embrace all that you are becoming because, YOU'VE ONLY BEGUN TO SHINE!

NOTES

NOTES

In the universe there is an immeasurable, indescribable force
which Shamans call intent and
absolutely everything that exists in the entire cosmos
is attached to intent by a connecting link.

Carlos Castaneda

Chapter 6

The Power of Intent

Have you ever considered the extraordinary value of setting a clear intent for success? I'd like to share with you how powerful I believe your intent is.

Consider intent to be setting the direction of your internal compass. Once direction is determined, it will serve as the constant reminder of where you're headed. As in most journeys, there will be detours obstacles, and traffic jams. However there will always be an alternative route. While detours happen, unexpected opportunities will also pop up as well as unexpected distractions. Carefully examine these, because sometimes each comes forth disguised as the other. One must question the value and relevance of both in order to determine the benefit toward fulfilling your goal. Is this the right moment to seize the opportunity or could it be saved for another time?

Another thing to consider is the quality of our intent. My experience with feeling successful in all my endeavors has shown me that when my intent is pure and flows from the heart with no ulterior motive or hidden agenda, anything is possible.

How do we maintain this crystal clear quality? One way is by crafting a personal mission statement (PMS) that will help you underscore your intent.

A PMS is a self-fulfilling declaration. By reading your PMS repeatedly, you will consciously and subconsciously be nurturing it until it has manifested in your life. Imagine how powerful that is?

This mission statement can be laminated and placed into your wallet or pocketbook, placed under your car visor, mounted on the wall in your office or attached to the bathroom mirror.

When crafting a PMS, make it engaging. Be prepared to make and keep this commitment to your transformation. Keep it reasonable as this shift can be monumental. This first small step is all it takes to bring forth noticeable change over time. Although this requires discipline and focus, it's manageable in order to keep things simple.

I'll give you an example of my current mission statement. It's posted in all the aforementioned places so it can't be missed. There have been times however I must consciously remind myself, it must actually be read to be effective! This may seem obvious until you think of all the things one can look at but not see as we go to and from work and our daily routines. A conscious effort must be made to ensure this does not happen. My personal mission statement reads as follows:

I am thriving financially doing what I love ~ writing, speaking professionally, and inspiring people to fulfill their greatness potential! I am a gardener; I plant the seeds of potential in everyone I encounter. I am also attracting key people to work with in forming partnerships of success. With the support of my success team, I am continually discovering my potential. I can no longer conceive any boundary to the probability of successful outcomes in all I pursue. Fueled by a passion to manifest a positive change in humanity, I lead with my heart, and I am able to teach others to use the same tools to fulfill their highest potential. My life is full of great health, peace, love and abundance.

There is no limit to the power of your mission statement beyond the limitations you set upon yourself. I have found the following helpful reminders.

- Consider setting the intent to keep clearly focused on your desired outcome.

- Practice discernment; don't completely dismiss an opportunity just because it doesn't fit into your plan now, as it may in the future. Reserve the right to get back to it another time.

- Remember how powerful your intent is!

- Be proud of your accomplishments thus far!

- Keep fine-tuning your timeline to success.

- Continue to see how your goal will positively impact those you share your story with!

- Date your PMS.

- Remember how powerful you are!

To begin drafting your PMS, start by listing what is most important to you. Is it more freedom, happiness, more money, better health? Also consider how your life will be once you attain what you goal. Get a pencil and take a few moments to explore the following.

The things most important to me are:

_____

_____

_____

_____

_____

_____

_____

My life, once I have achieved a goal (looks) (feels) (sounds) like:

_____

_____

_____

_____

_____

The thing I find most fulfilling about my life now is:

_____

_____

_____

_____

_____

_____

_____

You may find this exercise beneficial to do multiple times as you reach various milestones. An eraser is helpful for fine tuning, or changing your mind. Remember that you have the power to create the life you wish manifest.

Once you've crafted your statement remember to place it in several areas so you can see it often.

NOTES

THE POWER OF INTENT

Your work is to discover your work and then,
with all your heart, to give yourself to it.

—Buddha

Chapter 7

Accountability

What has changed for you since the exercise in the last chapter? When I began following the practice of repeating a self-affirming mantra and/or reading out loud my PMS faithfully on a daily basis, everything changed. My self-esteem grew, my posture became more erect, and I moved more gracefully. For the men reading - moving with grace equates to eloquence or confident motion. You will move with intent and confidence commanding the attention of those in your presence.

I challenge you to not let a day go by without reaffirming your belief in yourself and your abilities. An extraordinary thing will happen; you will become that which you affirm.

Now that we have begun to embody confidence, how do we keep the momentum going during busy, distracting or difficult times?

We hold the momentum by holding ourselves personally accountable. The theme of accountability lies very close to my heart, particularly personal accountability. How we hold ourselves accountable is quite subjective and not spoken of often. When the topic arises, our personal experience may not be what comes to mind immediately. I'm willing to bet our political or business leaders are the first things you think of.

Lack of accountability is more prevalent in society now than it has ever been. How can we make a difference? And why should we? Because leading by example is paramount for the sake of you, you're family and all of those in your current circle of influence.

My next question to you is this: to whom do you hold yourself accountable? For some it's ultimately their creator, for others it's our family, and for some it's never been considered. For me, it's a combination of things. Certainly my family is at the top of the list, but I also feel accountable to those I have shared my dreams with. I have mentors, my associates in Toastmasters International and the National Speakers Association, friends, family and my fellow visionaries.

In the past, not sharing my vision was a curse; merely holding me accountable to Leslie wasn't enough. I have realized I can be just as good at talking myself out of something as I can be talking myself into it. I became the master of a "good explanation", until the explanations began sounding like excuses; at which point, I stopped making excuses and simply began to make things happen. When things get tough we become challenged in uncomfortable ways and seemingly at the most inconvenient times. Excuses are always easier; it's like a note from your mother to leave school early or your bank letting you skip a loan payment. Sooner or later it all catches up with you, so why not deal with it now and move forward?

Moving beyond excuses, I decided one of the most instrumental things I could do was to put my intent "out there" and let the magic of coincidence otherwise known as synchronicity start happening. Amazingly, I began meeting people in my desired profession i.e. writers and speakers everywhere I turned. They were literally coming out of the woodwork! This will happen for you too, you must believe it is possible and it will happen.

Incredible as this was, it did not move me closer toward holding myself accountable to my dreams. I still needed help. I found a small group of like-minded people who shared a vision of moving toward their dreams as I did. They were just as serious about accountability as I was and when we were all willing to make the commitment to step up to the plate, be in support of one another, while following the path to our success.

I would strongly encourage you to develop a support structure. Ask your friends and business associates who they know that has traveled the path you are beginning. Chances are they know someone and would be happy to make an introduction. Initially, making time for another engagement may seem like "one more commitment" to fit into an already busy schedule, but I guarantee you - there's nothing quite like the enthusiasm of another positive person, or a group with similar goals and a shared vision.

It's now time to set your goals. Begin small; don't start out by overwhelming yourself with unrealistic expectations. Be aware that big goals may have to be broken down into manageable milestones. These milestones are critical to maintain momentum; our desired outcome is manifesting success not creating more challenges.

One thing you must consider when deciding on your goals is this: is this ultimately self-serving or will it make a positive impact on others? For some there is no higher calling than being of service to others regardless of the venue.

Let's get moving and make some progress! I like working with a large piece of paper to sort out my thoughts, the bigger the paper the larger and less limiting the ideas are. When I have all my thoughts written down, it makes it much easier to begin refining my goals. Refining means to simplify and make easier to understand, remember and recall. Perhaps something you could recite during a 30 second elevator ride. Leave no question as to what your mission is - a fifth grader ought to be able to understand it. For starters, let's get the basics down on paper or saved electronically. No holding back now!

Look back at your insight from Chapter 2. How can you take your vision and break it into three milestones? Inevitably you will break these three things down even further, but this is your starting point. Don't forget to refer to your declarations in Chapter 4, "I believe I am capable of...".

Take a moment and outline three attainable goals you have in mind for the next year.

Goal Number 1:

_____

_____

_____

Goal Number 2:

_____

_____

_____

Goal Number 3:

_____

_____

_____

We've discussed the importance of someone believing in you and the importance of being held accountable for your goals. I'm now suggesting we take this to the next level and find some successful people to assist you.

Think for a moment about some of the most successful people you know. How is service part of their business? How have they made an impact on you or society?

Make a list of the ten most successful people you know, their phone numbers, and the next time you are going to speak to them.

1. Name_____ Phone_____
   Date of next contact_____

2. Name_____ Phone_____
   Date of next contact_____

3. Name_____ Phone_____
   Date of next contact_____

4. Name_____ Phone_____
   Date of next contact_____

5. Name_____ Phone_____
   Date of next contact_____

6. Name_____ Phone_____
   Date of next contact_____

7. Name_____ Phone_____
   Date of next contact_____

8. Name_____ Phone_____
   Date of next contact_____

9. Name_____ Phone_____
   Date of next contact_____

10. Name_____ Phone_____
    Date of next contact_____

How many people on this list have the potential to become a mentor or connect you to a potential mentor? Schedule time to make some phone calls and find out.

Now make a list of the professional organizations you are a member of.

1. _____

2. _____

3. _____

4. _____

5. _____

How many of these organizations compliment the goals you have outlined? You may find the need to expand your network. Fortunately there are professional organizations for every conceivable type of business. Many times these organizations are seeking new members. I'd recommend volunteering or serving on a committee to facilitate getting to know the other members within an organization, you may find a mentor in the process.

These are the organizations I need to investigate:

1. _____

2. _____

3. _____

Just for fun, hold the image of reliable, trustworthy people finding <u>you</u> to work with in making your business or venture a success.

Mark your calendar when you began holding this image of reliable, trustworthy people finding you. Then track how quickly these people find you as well has how frequently they appear. You may be surprised how well this works!

Next we'll discuss turning your goals into manageable stepping-stones, paving your path to success!

NOTES

The problem with doing nothing
is not knowing when you're finished.

Benjamin Franklin

Chapter 8

Map To Manifestation

We've discussed getting our ideas down on paper and taking another step closer to manifesting our dreams. Could you find a piece of paper large enough to list your wealth of ideas and creative intention? How about a roll of Tyvek house wrap, it comes 3' x 165' or 9' x 100' for the really daring! Why not?!

Now that you've laid the foundation by discovering your first insight in Chapter 2 and outlined three goals in Chapter 7, what's next? How do we begin paving our way toward success? I cannot say enough about the power of our intent. Intent is the oxygen that fuels the fire within you. Most things need air to survive. You not only fuel the fire by which you create, but you also illuminate your path. This fire is your torch within and will show you an endless array of possibilities. The flame may dim from time to time however if you remain firm and strong in your convictions the flame will never go out.

While protocol is important, refined intent is critical, and has incredible purity much like unconditional love. Intent goes hand in hand with putting your idea "out there". You intend to succeed, and by seeing the outcome or imagining your success, you are taking one of the easiest steps toward manifesting the future you desire.

Now let's take a look at your three goals in Chapter 7. I'd like you to look at them from the point of creating a time line to move toward completion. If it seems in any way intimidating (you would be in good company), let's try a unique approach.

Find another big piece of paper and divide it into several sections as follows (or use the space below):

When I have a minute:

_____

_____

_____

_____

When I have an hour:

_____

_____

_____

_____

When I have an evening:

_____

_____

_____

_____

When I have a full day:

_____

_____

_____

_____

When I have a full week:

_____

_____

_____

_____

Now take a look at your three goals and decide if any of these ideas fit into these parameters without breaking them down into smaller steps. Chances are some may be refined enough to put into immediate action steps but more likely the goals are still too abstract. This is exactly the outcome we need for this exercise! If the three goals you've listed all work together – terrific. If they follow three different directions then select the most meaningful to you at the moment. This is the one we'll work on first. We'll be getting back to this timeline a little later.

Now let's take your goal and presume you are already there. Sometimes when planning things, I look at them in reverse order- I'm already here, what did I do in order to be properly prepared for this outcome? Just like going on vacation and packing our suitcases, we have a good idea of what we'll be doing and what we'll need, so we plan accordingly. If you were going on vacation but did not know your destination, wouldn't you have a hard time preparing? Ladies and Gentlemen, we are packing our suitcase for success.

You know that favorite outfit you like to wear on special occasions; does it need to be dry-cleaned? Is your passport current? Do you need any updated vaccinations for traveling to exotic locations? Who will water your house plants? All of these are important questions that need your consideration prior to going on vacation. We are now shifting into the mindset of looking at the pieces of a puzzle, the puzzle being our dream and the pieces are the stepping-stones paving the way.

There's a good chance that your idea is something you have never done before. You may not be sure of some of the things you need to do. There's also a chance that you may not have any idea what steps you need to take. That's okay. You have decided on your destination, the first and most important element. The rest of the puzzle pieces will come through asking questions of others that have traveled a similar path or by seeking out other successful people you admire. Perhaps some library or Internet research will be necessary or other sources like the Small Business Administration, a professor at a local community college, the local Chamber of Commerce or a related agency in your area. Start asking questions right away. Perhaps join an organization dedicated to people or businesses in the same field, imagine you belong in that group and are welcomed warmly.

Now, let's get back to our windows of time. Just in case you're asking yourself "What can I possibly accomplish in 5 minutes?" consider this. The imagination when used on a regular basis can fine-tune the art of daydreaming in any window of time you grant it. So be it 5, 15, or 30 minutes, practice stretching your imagination.

Here's how we'll begin. Take your chosen goal; think on it about what you have done to arrive at that outcome. This will be a combination of your research and the advice of those with whom you have spoken. These small steps or manageable bites will begin the sequence of events getting you toward your desired outcome. So often times when setting goals, we are terrific in the long-term concept but need encouragement to take the first few steps. The important part of this exercise is to consider how we are going to get from point A to point B. How aggressively we move through each step depends on many things, and it will be different for everyone. If you are working with a buddy or a group, please resist the temptation to compare yourself to them. Remember that they are mentoring you. We are all on different paths with different timelines and we all have unique gifts.

As you recognize these steps you need to take, place them in your "window of time" chart. Make your steps realistic because that will keep things manageable. I highly recommend using a pencil because you'll detect a change in your awareness of how to proceed many times before completing the exercise and you may need an eraser!

Remember to reward yourself for your successes, the goal is to encourage forward momentum and keep it going.

Congratulate yourself on taking action! Feeling great about the journey ahead is important because incredible things are coming your way! Next we will continue to fine tune the phases of our journey through the maps we are establishing.

NOTES

What we love to do
we find time to do.

John L. Spaulding

Chapter 9

Finding Time

Now that we've developed a map, how do we keep the momentum? We <u>make</u> time to maintain the momentum instead of letting other things distract us that simply fill our time.

Moving dreams through the manifestation process can be intimidating! I'd prefer not to call it work because that implies less than an enjoyable experience. So let's call it creative play! When something is right, it has a tendency to flow. Although there may be times when we feel challenged, our ability to move through the obstacle speaks volumes to the commitment we've made to fulfill our vision.

We've explored some of the basic steps required to move forward. Synchronicity has probably played a part in some pertinent discoveries and helped you meet some incredible people. If, for some reason things do not flow easily, then step back a moment and reexamine the goal. Connecting with your life's purpose is not difficult when you are headed in the right direction.

Let's presume that you've made some great connections, received timely information and are now accomplishing small goals within your timeline. The evolution of any process must be continually nourished with your time and focus. Even when something flows well, it will not maintain continuity of momentum without your direct participation.

Consider how we embrace a timeline for most of the tasks in our lives. Following a dream is no different. For starters, we are already accustomed to holding ourselves accountable with our daily routines of family and work life. Carving out a niche of time for yourself may not be easy or comfortable at first, especially if it's totally new to you. However, once you begin to do it I guarantee you'll enjoy it, get better at it and make it a priority in your life. I'm not talking about evading responsibilities. Everything requires balance. You will find the appropriate balance in time; some of us find it faster than others. As you continue to manifest, what brings you balance may also shift. For me regaining balance varies from being in silence to listening to music, acupuncture, a great massage, gardening or dancing. It depends on the intensity of where I am in the process.

Do you ever wish you were a busier person? Either you are smiling or rolling your eyes about now…..Many of us lead hectic lives already, and are capable of being distracted and falling off the "progress wagon." Being too busy can leave little energy to invest in following your dream. Your commitments to family and work are paramount however, examine where your time is invested beyond that. You may not consider making downtime as something productive, but consider this – down time renews the senses. Look for those mindless timewasters, like flipping through TV channels. Could your time be better utilized? You may have opportunities disguised within a daily routine where there are possibilities for renewing, by merely shifting your perception. For example, as much as I dislike multi-tasking, I have found that my commute time can be extremely productive. Sometimes I will listen to a motivational CD, music or sometimes nothing and revel in the silence of my thoughts. Some of my brightest ideas have been born on the road.

Now that you've already begun cultivating these terrific ideas and started filling in your timeline, have you noticed the big blocks of time are the easiest part? We have grandiose thoughts and visions, which seem so far away it makes them easier to entertain. Somehow that "big picture" timeframe is a great bridge to our dreams- which are under perpetual construction. Yet when it comes down to asking ourselves "what can I do today?" Oftentimes we cannot conceive of anything productive coming from 15 or 20 minutes. I've been down that road more times than I care to admit.

Let me say this about a quality block of time in small doses. When you are feeling like you need some encouragement or you are faced with a challenge and need to pick up the phone for emotional reinforcement a 10 or 15-minute conversation with a confidant can help immensely. Everyone is capable of tuning out the world for 15 minutes. If I can find 15 minutes, so can you.

I'd suggest keeping a notepad or digital recorder handy for that "inspiration" on the fly. Sometimes things will come to you that make no sense whatsoever, don't dismiss them; they will be relevant at some point on your journey. For such ideas, may I suggest a "good idea" jar? I like to place things to be considered at a later date in there for safekeeping. My jar is pretty full right now and I take comfort in knowing that all of those ideas are there for me when I am ready to invest time into them.

The process of researching your next steps and staying within your timeline will take an investment on your part; trust in your progress regardless of how small a step you take-as long as you take a step forward you are on the right track. If you are an instant gratification kind of person and have a need to see some progress FASTER, keep reading!

Have you ever heard of a dream board? It's a collage of photographs you've taken, photographs you clipped from magazines, perhaps words and phrases from newspapers basically anything that inspires you, or moves you, or grabs your attention. These images are things you desire, things you'll want to do, or do more often, or who you want to be, once you reach your goal. It need not be a 3' x 2' board, but it certainly could be. I like to use a piece of corkboard; its 3' x 4' and I keep it in my kitchen right next to the refrigerator. What a wonderful reminder of how I see myself spending my time and money in the future. This is a really fun, feel good exercise. Does this appeal to you?

Make a commitment to craft a dream board; you can do this in as little as 15 minutes. You may add things to it as often as you wish. The best part is realizing you've attained something on the board, removing the photograph and replacing it with another.

My dream board will be hung: _____

_____

_____

_____

_____

I have used clippings and photographs from the following publications:

_____

_____

_____

_____

_____

I'd suggest you place the date you assembled your dream board somewhere on it. Then as you manifest what you've placed on the board note the date. Are you manifesting your dreams faster than you anticipated?

Keep playing with the timeline and look for creative ways to carve out a niche of time. Perhaps while on the treadmill, you could focus on one element of your list or perhaps while cooking dinner. Food prep is an art form, and creativity breeds more creativity. Perhaps while gardening, as you nurture your plants, imagine you are nurturing yourself and your dream. Set your intent beforehand that this will be your creative playtime and that an idea will come to you. It doesn't need to be the whole enchilada. Be specific in your intent and focus on a small element to assure success. If you set the stage for something more complex than you are allotting time for, you may not have the results you desire. This is about small successes and moving forward.

NOTES

"If you surrender completely to the moments as they pass, you live more richly those moments."

Anne Morrow Lindbergh

Chapter 10

The Wisdom of Surrender

What do you think of when you hear the word surrender?

For the longest time I thought of weakness, inadequacy, resignation or just plain "giving up"! Over the years my perception has shifted. When I hear the term "surrender" I am now compelled to offer my congratulations to the individual who crossed a barrier to his or her own progress. Surrender means letting go of something that is holding us back from attaining a new higher level of excellence. It means to decide or to admit to yourself that what you thought was a high priority is no longer the highest priority. Presently, to me, surrender implies strength, perseverance and a willingness to sacrifice something in order to move forward. It means accepting <u>what is</u>, that we cannot change.

There once was a time I'd resist any interruption or change in direction, unless it was my idea. I'd most often strongly resist and with a bad attitude. I'd never give any thought to the compatibility of the plan with my present circumstance; my mind was set, end of story. The consideration of an alternative solution to the problem being presented, or the simple notion that I may be in the wrong place at the wrong time, never occurred to me.

How does this pertain to surrender? Think of the phrase, "If you can't beat 'em, join 'em". Surrender isn't anything new in the realm of personal growth, however misperceptions are common.

Pride and ego play a large part in our inability to surrender. Either through our upbringing or our conditioning, we believe we are entitled to certain returns on intellectual, mental, emotional or physical investments. When our expectations are not delivered, we can become disappointed, frustrated and eventually apathetic. Can you imagine going through an entire day without having your ego present?

What if we began to understand that our experience is the lesson, regardless of the outcome? We view every experience as something we were meant to have. What kind of shift would that create in your day-to-day thinking? Perhaps you would not be so easily aggravated when you're stuck behind a slow driver or you miss that green light, or are in the slowest checkout lane at the supermarket if you're running late.

When something occurs that's out of your control, how do you respond? Do you fight back with anger and frustration or do you step back, assess the situation, and think clearly about any alternatives to enable you to continue to reach your goal? Frustration often leads to blame, which frequently deteriorates further. Our response is completely under our control even if the situation is not. We decide what it means. Instead of asking, "why must I endure this?" Instead ask, "what is good for me in this? What opportunity do I now have?" If you persist, you will find answers. Assessing blame merely passes the responsibility for one's behaviors and actions to someone else, victimizing yourself as well.

Surrender does <u>not</u> mean to give up or give in, but rather it is a form of acceptance, enabling a fresh outlook on the situation. Surrender allows us to see the lesson in our dilemma and move forward with our lives. Examine a week in your life. Note when your plan changed and note if the outcome was better than your original expectation. Do you notice a pattern?

Original plan: _____

_____

_____

_____

_____

Altered plan:

_____

_____

_____

_____

_____

My attitude before I accepted the altered plan:

_____

_____

_____

_____

_____

My attitude after I accepted the altered plan:

_____

_____

_____

_____

_____

What could I have done differently? _____

_____

_____

_____

_____

Surrender doesn't mean giving up or giving in. It is just the acknowledgement of the situation. <u>Surrender is the gift of a new perspective</u>!!

We've all heard the phrase "resistance is futile" however, most of us do not apply it directly to our circumstances, especially when the circumstance first arises. Usually we are not the only one involved, and the acceptance of a situation requires others to embrace the change as well. We then become ambassadors for change.

How well we embrace this role is key. We have the ability to inspire others with our words; however our actions and responses are watched more closely than we think. Body language conveys a much stronger message than our words. Make sure your inward self is reflected by outward actions that match.

If your actions do not match, change your inner self until your automatic responses do match. If you try to merely change your actions, you will invariably miss something. The power of this comes from deep within. When you find and embrace the opportunities stemming from the changes, your words and actions will line up.

Being angry and frustrated takes much more energy than being accepting of a situation. That anger could be better channeled into making positive change following unexpected circumstance. This change could enable one to manifest a different and perhaps a more profound outcome.

There will always be circumstances outside our control. These situations we'd love to have a handle on but never will, while others may not willingly embrace the concept of surrender. However once we have accepted a situation, we have chosen to engage the first tool of change. We are all conveyors of a similar message with different vehicles for delivery. Engage your optimism, extend your vision beyond your immediate circumstance and foster the next step forward.

As you master the art of surrender, you will notice others around you that thrive on resistance. You may wonder how you never noticed this before. Choose wisely with whom you spend your time. Everyone will want to know the secret to your serenity and level-headedness.

Consider keeping a log of the circumstances that required you to shift your direction or perspective. Do the outcomes routinely produce better results than your original plan? Has your stress level reduced significantly in these situations?

Congratulations, you are becoming a more serene person and are becoming an expert on mastering the art of surrender.

NOTES

*"Be the change you want
to see in the world."*

Mahatma Gandhi

Chapter 11

The Impact of Optimism

Are you mindful of the tremendous impact being positive has your well-being? Possessing an optimistic, confident outlook is so important! Consider evaluating how you maintain your optimism and develop a plan to keep that process a priority. Let's look at the following examples, write down what you may be thinking if the following happened to you.

When I am stuck in traffic, I view the delay as:

_____

_____

_____

_____

When an appointment I am looking forward to is canceled or postponed I think:

_____

_____

_____

_____

When an object dear to me is broken or lost my first reaction is:

_____

_____

_____

_____

There are many ways to view each of these circumstances. Imagine a positive spin to each of these scenarios. Being stuck in traffic or behind the slowest driver in existence could be keeping you out of harm's way. When an appointment is cancelled at the last moment, you have just been given a gift of time to do with as you wish; make the most of it. When something is lost or broken, it may have served its usefulness to you and this loss is making room for something at least equally wonderful or better. Knowing how to have a positive perspective is one of the most important skills we develop in our lifetime. As we cultivate optimism, we will seek out and bring like-minded people into our lives.

What we choose to expose ourselves to also has an impact on the level of our optimism. If we allow it, the media can have such an influence on our emotional and mental well-being. Do you feel empowered or inspired after watching TV or listening to the news? Of course it depends on the programming but I'm guessing not. By choice I don't have cable or satellite TV, nor do I read the newspaper. I will listen to NPR from time to time but am very selective in the programming. While staying informed and current is one thing, being disheartened over an abundance of bleak news is another.

We need to remember that our mind is constantly being programmed with whatever we choose to feed it. My preference is listening to uplifting individuals who inspire me. Imagine how beneficial it can be to hear an inspirational speaker! It's like having your own personal coach on call that can give you that necessary inspirational "Shot in the arm".

Let's take a look at the people you spend the most time with. Are they encouraging, nurturing empowering and uplifting? Or are they negative and filled with pessimism they claim is realism? Consider making a list of the pleasant, happiest people you know and then, spend time with them. Maintaining a positive mindset is easier when those around you compliment you with similar mindsets.

Even with text messaging and e-mailing there may be times you need a quick "pick me up" but your optimistic friends are not available. So think of a few things that brings you joy. Inventory these memories on a brightly colored index card. Then on the other side make a list of what you like about yourself or what others have told you they like about you. Precede your attributes with, "I am a terrific". When the need strikes, take out the card, read your affirmations aloud, then repeat as necessary.

These things bring me joy:

_____

_____

_____

_____

I am terrific because I:

_____

_____

_____

_____

Keep this card with you at all times. Every time you recite these affirmations I guarantee you'll feel better, feel empowered, and that will keep moving closer to your life's calling!

NOTES

"The strongest statements are made without saying a word."

(recent Chrysler ad)

Chapter 12

Walk Your Talk

Do you know anyone that talks a good line, but when your back is turned their actions are not in line with their words? For some, it's an easy trap to fall into, for others, it may not be easy but it still happens. This is your opportunity to bring together all the topics presented up to this point. Reading a good book or sharing your insight with a friend is a good place to start; but actions always speak louder than words. The most important thing you can do is determine how serious you are about moving forward, and how passionate you are about manifesting change in your life.

This is where so many folks become intimidated. We have all had a terrific idea that didn't go anywhere at some point in our lives. Some adverse circumstance could've been empowered – perhaps through fear - then excuses were made and we did not following through.

Our ego and our past experiences do not always work in our favor, especially when we aim high. Is your idea so amazing that it's never been done or heard of before? If so, excellent. I am excited for you! What a terrific opportunity to motivate others while we break down barriers. When I get one of those inspirations, I immediately put it on paper or put the concept on a digital recorder. There's nothing quite like listening to yourself filled with excitement to revive your mood if doubt creeps in. Sometimes we are our own best motivational speakers.

The inception phase of any idea is the catalyst for change. Go with it for as long as you can. Don't hesitate to shut off your cell phone, skip dinner or lose a little sleep. Ride the wave of creativity and inspiration as long as you possibly can. Your investment will be returned to you tenfold. If you know any creative people, you may have already witnessed this phenomenon and can appreciate its power.

Now that you have your insight/extraordinary idea and determined where and when you are most creative, you've established the foundation for your success combined with the belief in your abilities, the acceptance of your gifts and understanding the power of your intent you've created the framework to bring your dreams to life. You've begun to understand that holding yourself accountable, making time to nurture your dream and maintain optimism in the face of a challenge will not only continue to empower you, it will empower those around you. Imagine the byproduct of your thoughts and actions as an inspiration to others. You have projected success and are attaining it. Have you asked yourself the following questions yet?

When do I see myself in this role? What am I wearing to be "dressed for success"? How do I feel physically, mentally and emotionally about bringing this to fruition? What are the people closest to me saying, as they congratulate me on my success?

I see myself in this role by (date):

_____

_____

_____

_____

When I execute this plan, I am wearing:

_____

_____

_____

_____

I can now see myself:

_____

_____

_____

_____

Knowing I have brought this to fruition I feel physically:

_____

_____

_____

_____

_____

Mentally I think and feel:

_____

_____

_____

_____

_____

Emotionally I think and feel:

_____

_____

_____

_____

_____

The song of success sounds like:

_____

_____

_____

_____

_____

My family and closest friends are telling me:

_____

_____

_____

_____

Moving forward, let's print out some calendar pages month by month throughout the next year. Examine your work and familial responsibilities; enter them on the calendar as best you can, then determine where you can dedicate time to your dream.

Take a moment and schedule time to develop your concept if you haven't already. Only you know your peak moments of creativity, make time around them. Will it be helpful to consider who you influence through manifesting this dream and how will you inspire them? Have you asked yourself how important this project is? Do you need to arrange time off work? Do you need to involve your family?

You are the master gardener of this vision. You've prepared the soil, planted the seeds and have enhanced the germination process. <u>Your</u> intent and <u>your</u> enthusiasm are the sun and the water. Your enthusiasm will become contagious; you will engage and inspire others. By putting into the universe your vision, you will be calling in other master gardeners to assist you and offer advice. You'll be surprised how many people are out there willing to help. It's almost as if they've been waiting for you to ask. You may hear comments such as "I always knew you were a visionary, I am happy to help any way I can" or "What a wonderful idea, you will inspire so many with your enthusiasm". The impact of your dream is endless.

Walk your talk, and embody what you are about to become! Statements such as *I wish, I think, I want, I will, I need* are not as powerful to the psyche as *I am*. Before I began this path of writing and speaking, I can remember sitting with a group of people, few of which I knew. Everyone took a turn stating who they were and what they did. I made the mistake of claiming that I was "becoming" an author and speaker. My new friend turned to me with a stern facial expression and stated "you said that incorrectly." Immediately I knew what he meant and revised my statement to "I *am* an author/speaker." That was incredibly empowering and the more I repeated it the more powerful it became.

What is your mantra for success?

Please accept my congratulations on your progress thus far. In working through the exercises in this book you've taken your destiny into your own hands. You are well on your way through one of the most incredible journeys you'll ever make – as you learn to Tap Your Source!

NOTES

In Summary

It was my sole intent to introduce a new perspective on an old, oftentimes painful concept - transition. My hope is that if for only a moment; people could entertain the possibility of something extraordinary coming out of something deemed otherwise unpleasant-then an amazing shift could occur. A shift that would not only affect the individual at the forefront of change but perhaps creating a shift that would affect generations to come.

How we see and carry ourselves radiates well beyond us. It travels beyond our families and into our communities. We have much more power than we give ourselves credit for. In growing through our own challenges we inspire others to greatness. We may never fully know the realm of our influence, however. If we imagine that every success we have is also a familial and a communal success – can you imagine the impact that could have? It is our duty to inspire our children, our spouses and our friends. It is my duty to inspire you.

Many blessings go out to you and yours throughout the incredible journey of discovering your true potential. May you have a positive impact on everyone you encounter as you embrace and Tap Your Source.

Success consists of going from failure to failure
without loss of enthusiasm.

Winston Churchill

www.ingramcontent.com/pod-product-compliance
Lightning Source LLC
Chambersburg PA
CBHW080519110426
42742CB00017B/3166